TAKE TEN YEARS

1900s

THE FIRST TEN YEARS

MARGARET SHARMAN

Evans

EVANS BROTHERS LIMITED

D0279765

Contents

Introduction – Theme chart for the first decade   **6 – 7**

1900 In South Africa, the Boer War continues for the third year. Mafeking is freed from its siege. The Boxers in China besiege foreigners in Peking, until help arrives. A West African colony revolts.   **8 – 11**

1901 The Queen's death brings to an end the 'Victorian Age'. In the United States a president is shot. The new president, Theodore Roosevelt, begins to reform monopolies. Australia joins the British empire.   **12 – 15**

1902 King Edward VII is crowned in Westminster Abbey. The Russians look for a new 'sphere of influence'. The Boer War ends. The United States suffers from a miners' strike.   **16 – 18**

1903 Travellers learn new ways of getting about – in cars, airships, and even the new invention, the aeroplane. There is research into the lives of the poor in England and America. Pope Pius X is crowned.   **19 – 22**

1904 Russia invades Korea, and Japan goes to war with Russia. France and Britain become friends after many years of suspicion. Captain Scott explores the Antarctic. The British invade Tibet.   **23 – 25**

1905 A revolution breaks out in Russia, as its army and navy are defeated in the Far East. The German Kaiser seeks new allies. Women protest at not having the vote.   **26 – 28**

1906 World-wide earthquakes and volcanic eruptions cause much destruction. The *Dreadnought* is launched from Plymouth. Africans in Tanganyika rebel against European occupation.   **29 – 31**

1907 Leopold II loses the Congo to his government. American battleships circle the globe. Mr. Pierpont Morgan saves the United States from economic disaster. South Africa passes a race law. 32 – 34

1908 The Turkish empire has a new parliament and constitution. There is a crisis in the Balkans. Sir Arthur Evans discovers the palace of Knossos. Unemployed British workers stage a hunger march. 35 – 38

1909 The first Old Age Pensions are paid in Britain, but a new budget is rejected. Riots lead to a 'Tragic Week' in Spain. Turkey and the Balkans are still unsettled. Immigrants to the United States swell the population. 39 – 41

People of 1900–1909 42 – 43

For the first time ever 44 – 45

New words and expressions 45

Glossary 46

Further reading 46

Index 47

The pictures on page 4 show
British troops in the Boer War
Paris exhibition 1900
Queen Victoria
The Tsar of Russia, Nicholas II
The *Dreadnought*

The pictures on page 5 show
City Hall, San Francisco, damaged by the 1906 earthquake
A church damaged by riots in Spain
Robert Peary, explorer, with his wife and son
Turks in Constantinople, during the revolution
Louis Blériot lands at Dover

Introduction

In the first ten years of the twentieth century, many political events involved colonies or territories belonging to European powers. When the Boer War ended, South Africa was added to the huge British empire. The British were proud of their empire, and said 'the sun never sets on it' because it spread around the world. In 1901 Australia was admitted to it. The British government sought to protect empire trade by taxing imports from other countries.

Some colonies did not want to be ruled from overseas. The Ashanti of the Gold Coast almost succeeded in massacring the British governor and his wife. The Germans faced a rising in Tanganyika. In other parts of Africa, Morocco became a French mandate; and the misrule in the Belgian Congo was exposed.

In Europe, two Balkan states left the Turkish empire, and a new political party started the reform of Turkey. The Germans, French and British all tried to win spheres of influence, as they struggled for a balance of power. By 1909 Britain and Germany were arming as if for war.

Mount Vesuvius in Italy, and Mount Pelée in the Caribbean both erupted. There were major earthquakes in the United States, South America and Sicily; hundreds of people died. Those who were made homeless added to the great number of poor and starving people in Europe and the USA.

At this time America was everyone's idea of heaven. If things were bad in Russia, the Balkans, Ireland, or Japan, people thought about emigrating to what they saw as the land of opportunity. The boat fare was cheap, and immigrants thought that jobs were easy to get. This was not always so.

There was a great difference between rich and poor. Well-to-do people had fine houses and gardens, looked after by domestic servants and gardeners. There were nannies and governesses for the children. Though some young women were getting jobs, most stayed at home until they married. They did not have the vote.

In England, Queen Victoria was succeeded by her son Edward VII. He was a shrewd man, and very popular. In the United States, Theodore Roosevelt was one of the best presidents the country had ever had.

YEARS	WORLD AFFAIRS
1900	International force relieves Peking
1901	USA to govern Philippines Australia joins British empire Cause found for yellow fever
1902	Nations look for 'spheres of influence'
1903	Britain proposes free trade Panama becomes independent
1904	*Entente cordiale* between France and Britain
1905	Russians ally with Germany
1906	Morocco to be French mandate
1907	Congo Free State becomes Belgian Congo
1908	Turkish Sultan forced to appoint parliament Crisis in the Balkans
1909	

WARS & CIVIL DISOBEDIENCE	PEOPLE	EVENTS
Boer War in South Africa Boxer rebellion in China Ashanti rebel in West Africa	Davis and Ward win Davis Cup	Paris Exhibition held Olympic Games in France
	Queen Victoria dies President McKinley shot Tolstoy criticizes Russian government	Oil found in Texas
Boer War ends	King Edward VII crowned Kipling writes *Just So Stories*	Mount Pelée erupts The Aswan Dam is opened
	Henry Ford manufactures 'Model A' car Wright brothers take to the air James Whistler, artist, dies	New Pope crowned in Rome
War between Japan and Russia Dervishes fight British in Somaliland	Robert Falcon Scott explores Antarctica Roosevelt promises Americans a 'square deal' Bernard Shaw writes *Major Barbara*	British expedition to Tibet Olympic Games in United States
Revolution in Russia Japan wins war in Far East	Baroness Orczy writes *Scarlet Pimpernel* Father Gapon leads demonstrators to Winter Palace in Russia	Suffragettes ask for vote
Maji Maji rebellion in Tanganyika Villagers punished for Egyptian incident	Alfred Dreyfus reinstated in French army President Roosevelt wins Nobel prize	Mount Vesuvius erupts San Francisco destroyed by earthquake
	Mohandas Gandhi leads Indian protest Florence Nightingale honoured Darrow defends 'Big Bill' Haywood in Chicago	French workers demonstrate over wine prices Boy Scouts formed
	Asquith becomes Prime Minister Sir Arthur Evans discovers Knossos Mrs. Anderson is first British lady mayor	Olympic Games in London Earthquake in Sicily *Dreadnought* launched
Riots in Spain Young Turks take over in Turkey	Peary reaches North Pole Blériot flies Channel Marconi wins Nobel Prize	House of Lords rejects budget

1900

Jan 25   Boers win the Battle of Spion Kop
April 30   Fifth Paris Exhibition in full swing
July 22   Olympic Games end
Aug 14   Boxer rebellion defeated in China
July 14   British troops relieve Kumasi, Gold Coast

THE BOER WAR

BOERS TRAP BRITISH IN THREE TOWNS

Jan 6, Ladysmith, South Africa The British and the Boers (Dutch settlers, or Afrikaaners) both have provinces in South Africa. The Transvaal, a Boer province, has rich gold mines, where many British men are employed. The Boers tax them heavily, and the British government has objected. This is one of the quarrels that has caused this war. British troops have arrived from England, and both sides have suffered many casualties in the fighting.

The Boers have surrounded Ladysmith, the British military headquarters, and two other towns, Mafeking and Kimberley. Thousands of British soldiers and civilians, both black and white, are trapped in these towns. They are now short of food.

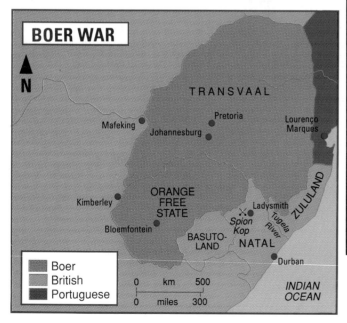

BLOODY BATTLE ON SPION KOP

Jan 25, Spion Kop, Natal Last night, after dark, 2000 British soldiers swarmed up a hill called Spion Kop, overlooking a tributary of the Tugela River. With their field guns they hoped to guard their troops as they crossed the river and marched towards Ladysmith, 25 kilometres (16 miles) away. But at daylight they were shocked to find that the Boers were on a higher spur of the hill. High explosive shells burst among them all day. As night fell, the remaining British soldiers retreated to the valley. Over 1500 men have died today on Spion Kop. Winston Churchill, a war correspondent, said: "Men were staggering along alone, or supported by comrades, or crawling on hands and knees, or carried on stretchers . . . I passed about two hundred as I was climbing up."

BRITISH ENTER MAFEKING

May 16, Mafeking British troops have ended the Boers' siege of Kimberley and Ladysmith. Today they marched into Mafeking. This little railway town was besieged by the Boers for seven months. The colonel in charge of the town, Robert Baden-Powell, has kept the enemy guessing. One of his deceptions was to make imitation guns out of wood. Young boys carrying these wooden guns marched round the town walls. From the Boer positions the weapons looked real, and they thought Mafeking was well defended.

The Boer War or South African War began in 1899. It is being fought by Dutch settlers, the Boers, against the English.

CROWDS IN ENGLAND REJOICE

May 21, London The 'relief' of Mafeking has been greeted in England with the greatest joy. There have been torchlight processions and street parties. Even young children are wild with excitement. A ten-year-old boy at boarding school has written to his mother: "On Saturday morning we heard a lot of shouting and all the boys wanted to know what it was, so after we had finished school Mr. Bridge [his teacher] read us out of the paper MAFEKING IS RELIEVED. We simply *yelled*."

The news of Mafeking's relief is announced on the stock exchange.

FOREIGNERS' ORDEAL IN CHINA

BOXERS KILL DIPLOMATS

June 20, Peking, China The German minister to China was today murdered in Peking. This follows the killing nine days ago of the Japanese Chancellor. Members of a Chinese secret society are murdering foreigners, and Chinese Christians. Europeans call them 'the Boxers', because of the rebels' belief that boxing and other exercises protect them from bullets.

The Chinese Empress Tzu Hsi approves of their actions. She, too, wants to get rid of 'foreign devils'. She has sent Chinese troops to besiege the legations. These diplomatic buildings are like a foreign walled town within Peking. About 900 foreign diplomats, their wives and their children, and 3000 Chinese Christians, are trapped there. All day the Boxers and Chinese troops shoot over the walls, and set fire to legation buildings. The besieged people are living on starvation rations. Every day they have to put out fires, build temporary shelters and care for the wounded.

An army of European, American and Japanese soldiers has set off from the coast by train to help them. They are due to arrive tonight.

SIEGE ENDS AS ARMY ARRIVES

Aug 14, Peking On June 21 the Empress declared war on all foreigners. Chinese soldiers destroyed a troop train at Tientsin, and the soldiers had to fight their way to Peking on foot. They have arrived just in time. In another day the Boxers would have broken into the legations. The Empress has fled from Peking. An eyewitness in one legation said: "By two o'clock every rifle that could be brought in line was replying to the enemy's fire. If this continued, in a couple of hours our ammunition would be exhausted, and we would have only our bayonets to rely on."

Italian soldiers guard Boxer prisoners. A combined European, American and Japanese army has put down the rebellion.

The fantasy 'illuminated palace' on the lake is a feature of the Exhibition.

LIGHTS DRAW CROWDS

April 30, Paris, France Buildings, fountains, and the River Seine have all been lit with the recently invented electric lighting for a fortnight now, to celebrate the Fifth Paris Exhibition. Many countries have put on displays. There is an English Tudor house, an Indian pavilion, and a Chinese pagoda. The exhibition also reminds us of all the wonderful inventions, arts and buildings of the last century. These include the Eiffel Tower, now ten years old. Already people are saying that this will be 'the exhibition of the century'.

FRENCH DOMINATE OLYMPICS

July 22, Paris The Olympic Games ended today. They were part of the Paris Exhibition. Events took place on bumpy grass and dirt roads. They were so informal that some of the winners did not realize they were competing in the Olympics; and a Dutch rowing crew invited a small French boy to act as cox, though he had never coxed before.

The French team was largest, with 884 competitors. They won the greatest number of medals. The United States sent their college and club teams. Ray Ewry (USA) was outstanding at the high and long jump. Women competed for golf and tennis medals.

The 500 metres takes place between trees and onlookers in a park in Paris.

GOVERNOR FLEES FROM BRITISH FORT

July 14, Kumasi fort, Gold Coast   Serious disturbances were reported in April from this British colony in West Africa. The British governor had angered the Ashanti tribe by asking for their Golden Stool. This huge chair, 200 years old, is the symbol of Ashanti unity. The Ashanti hid it, and besieged the British fort. The governor and his wife escaped from the fort three weeks ago. British troops, who arrived at Kumasi today, were too late to save hundreds of people who had starved to death.

WAR INFLUENCES THE ELECTION

Oct 17, London   The General Election has been fought with some bitterness. It is called the 'Khaki' election, because the Boer War is the main issue and the soldiers wear khaki uniforms. The Conservatives won. Their slogan, 'A vote for the Liberals is a vote for the Boers', angered the Liberals.

Lord Salisbury continues as Prime Minister.

NEWS IN BRIEF . . .

DAVIS RECEIVES HIS OWN TROPHY

Aug 10, Boston, USA   The American tennis players Dwight Davis and Holcombe Ward have won the first Davis Cup tournament. This is the competition which Dwight Davis himself set up six months ago!

GALES LASH BRITAIN

Dec 31, London   The year ends with storms all over the country. The Scottish fishing fleet is in difficulties, and 33 seamen have drowned. Lighthouse keepers in the Shetland Islands were swept away by high seas. Further south, one of the upright stones at Stonehenge, the ancient monument, was torn from the earth.

MORE HORSELESS CARRIAGES MANUFACTURED

Dec 1, New York   The United States now has 8000 cars on the roads. Over 1600 motor cars, driven by steam power, were manufactured this year. Another 1500 electric cars were on sale. And a new fuel, gasoline, is increasingly being used.

Just two of 30 designs of electric car made by a company in Chicago.

1901

Jan 1	Australia becomes a Commonwealth
Feb 2	Funeral of Queen Victoria of Britain
Mar 17	Cossacks halt riots in Russia
Sept 7	Chinese to pay for Boxer rising
Sept 14	Theodore Roosevelt becomes President of USA

THE QUEEN IS DEAD
END OF AN ERA

Jan 22, Osborne, Isle of Wight   The 'Victorian Age' is over. This morning Queen Victoria died at Osborne House on the Isle of Wight. She was 81. Few people can remember any other monarch, as she has ruled since 1837.

HORSES BREAK FREE AT FUNERAL

Feb 2, Windsor   The Queen's coffin arrived on this cold and windy morning by boat and train from the Isle of Wight. At Windsor railway station it was put on a gun-carriage. But one of the horses pulling the carriage reared up, and then both horses broke free. The naval guards had to pull the gun-carriage to Windsor Castle Chapel. Thousands of people lined the route. The Chapel bell tolled, and guns were fired at one-minute intervals. At the end of the service an official cried, "God Save the King!" A new era has begun.

> "It was eerie entering the half-dark Choir lit only by wax tapers – for it was a dull day – as we moved up to the altar rails, taking our places on the north side. From here we could see the Royal Box, in which were Queen Alexandra and the other Royal ladies in deep mourning . . . I received an official fee of half-a-crown [2s 6d] for singing, and with it I bought a photograph of the old Queen."
> Reminiscences of a Windsor choirboy

KING OPENS PARLIAMENT

Feb 14, London   King Edward VII and Queen Alexandra drove to Westminster today to open the new session of Parliament. Londoners are delighted to know that the King will perform such duties. Queen Victoria was seldom seen in public.

Changes are also being made to Windsor Castle, Buckingham Palace and Sandringham House, the royal residences. The King loves entertaining. He is modernizing the rooms and making them more comfortable for his guests.

ATTACK SHOCKS AMERICA

US PRESIDENT SHOT

Sept 5, Buffalo, New York In front of a shocked audience, President William McKinley was shot at as he held out his hand to his attacker. The President had been speaking on the need to trade with other countries. "Isolation is no longer possible or desirable," he said. After his speech people lined up to shake his hand. Among them was Leon Czolgosz, son of a Polish immigrant. He fired twice at the President, whose condition tonight is not thought to be serious.

The US President, William McKinley, is shot at close range by Leon Czolgosz.

ROOSEVELT SWORN IN

Sept 14, Buffalo, New York Vice-President Theodore Roosevelt was on a hunting holiday when he received news that President McKinley was dying from gunshot wounds. Today he has become, at 42, the youngest president of the United States.

AUTHOR BLAMED FOR RIOTS

March 17, St. Petersburg, Russia Leo Tolstoy, the author of *War and Peace*, is blamed for serious student riots in Moscow and St. Petersburg. Tolstoy has written against the government and against religion. Last year the Orthodox Church excommunicated him. Today the students were beaten back by mounted troops, the Cossacks, and hundreds have been arrested.

Leo Tolstoy

US SENDS GOVERNOR TO PHILIPPINES

July 4, Manila Judge William Howard Taft is the new Governor of the Philippines. For the past two years American troops have fought a guerrilla war against Filipinos, natives of the Philippines, who object to being part of an American colony. The Anti-Imperialist League in the US agrees with the Filipinos that no country should be ruled by another without its consent. The Filipino rebel leader, Emilio Aguinaldo, was captured in the mountains in May. Since then US troops have been withdrawn. Governor Taft is a sympathetic man, and is winning friends on the islands.

BOER CAMPS A DISGRACE

Aug 16, Cape Town The Boers in South Africa continue to fight guerrilla battles against British soldiers. Civilians, mainly women and children, have been providing Boers with food and clothing. To stop this, Lord Kitchener, Commander of the British forces, ordered that all civilians should be put into guarded camps. Many of their farms have been burnt, and the fields are full of dead animals, shot by British soldiers.

The camps are terrible places. There are no doctors or medical supplies, no blankets, and no proper sanitation. Water is very scarce. The inmates get less food than the soldiers do. Many are starving, and hundreds die from disease. People from Britain who have visited the camps are shocked by the conditions in which the Boers have to live.

CHINESE TO PAY FOR BOXER UPRISING

Sept 7, Peking The Chinese government has been ordered to pay a huge sum to the countries which raised the siege of Peking last year. The Americans say that half the money they receive will go to help Chinese students in the United States.

In China, two princes and three leading courtiers will be beheaded, and three officials have been ordered to commit suicide. Over a hundred other people will be punished. Empress Tzu Hsi will continue as ruler. The Chinese feel humiliated by the affair.

SINGLE TRACK IN DARKEST AFRICA

Dec 20, Mombasa Ten years ago the British government decided to build a railway from the coast of the East Africa Protectorate [now Kenya] to Uganda. Today the first locomotive steamed into the new railway station, Port Florence, on Lake Victoria. Laying the track has not been easy. Workers brought from India suffered from dysentery and malaria; some were even eaten by lions. The railway can carry both goods and passengers, opening up the fertile country along the line. Soon it will be farmed by British settlers.

BUSINESSMEN WARNED BY PRESIDENT

Dec 3, Washington President Roosevelt has spoken out against 'trusts' in American business. Trusts are formed when businesses join together, and have a monopoly in the goods they sell. The trust can then fix prices and wages because there is no competition. The President says trusts destroy small businesses. They also make a few men very rich.

LIBERAL MP THREATENED BY MOB

Dec 18, Birmingham Mr. David Lloyd George had a narrow escape tonight. An angry crowd braved the wintry weather to stop him speaking at the Town Hall. Gatecrashers surged into the hall with home-made weapons – bottles, bricks and cudgels – and a riot broke out in the street. Two people died and 40 were taken to hospital. Mr. Lloyd George made his escape dressed as a policeman. He is unpopular in this Conservative town because he speaks against the South African war.

Mr. David Lloyd George, the Welsh Liberal MP

NEWS IN BRIEF . . .

A LAND BATHED IN OIL

Jan 10, Texas, USA The oil that seeped out of the ground in Texas and spoiled crops is going to transform the country. Oil drillers today bored through rock and came to a layer of oil underneath. It rushed up to the surface in a great black fountain, shooting high into the sky. When it is under control, it will provide fuel for years to come, and make Texas rich.

NEW CONTROLS FOR DANGEROUS DISEASE

Aug 25, Havana, Cuba Now that we know that yellow fever is carried by mosquitoes, we can do something about it. The American Yellow Fever Commission says people should drain away still water, on which mosquitoes breed. They should cover pools with oil. These methods seem to be working. The terrible epidemics in Cuba may be coming to an end.

NEW COMMONWEALTH COUNTRY BORN

Jan 1, Sydney Australia enters the new century as the youngest commonwealth country in the British Empire – born today! Six Australian states have joined in a federal union. This is the first time in history that a whole continent has been occupied by one nation.

The celebrations in Sydney began with a procession through the streets to the pavilion (right) where a message from Queen Victoria was read out.

MARCONI'S MAGIC MOMENT MAY LEAD TO MORE

Dec 16, Poldhu, Cornwall The Italian inventor, Mr. Marconi, has made a breakthrough. He has succeeded in sending a signal by wireless telegraphy right across the Atlantic Ocean. The signal travelled from Cornwall to Newfoundland, a distance of over 3300 kilometres (2000 miles). The sound Mr. Marconi received was faint, but there is no doubt that his theory of transmitting messages through the air really works.

The inventor Mr. Guglielmo Marconi and his wireless apparatus

1902

May 8   **Mount Pelée erupts**
June 1   **The Boer War ends**
Aug 9   **King Edward VII of Britain crowned**
Oct 23   **Miners return to work in USA**
Dec 10   **The Aswan Dam is opened**

THE KING IS CROWNED

Aug 9, London   Choirboys from Windsor Castle, St. Paul's Cathedral, Westminster Abbey and the Chapel Royal joined together today to sing at the coronation of King Edward VII in Westminster Abbey. They watched, spellbound, as the distinguished guests entered the Abbey. The coronation was postponed last June because the King had to have an operation for appendicitis. This new operation is a serious one, but the King would have died without it.

Today the King seemed in good health. The Archbishop of Canterbury, however, who is 81 and nearly blind, had to have the prayers, printed in large letters, held up for him. He put the crown on the King's head with shaking hands.

King Edward VII's coach passes through Parliament Square on Coronation Day.

NATIONS SEEK ASIAN ALLIES

Jan 30, London   The major countries of the world are all eager to extend their power. They make friends with smaller countries, and often have naval or military bases there. These are their 'spheres of influence'.

The Japanese suggested that Manchuria should be Russia's 'sphere of influence', while Korea should be Japan's. The Chinese have already allowed Russia to build the Trans-Siberian Railway across Manchuria to the Russian port of Vladivostok. The Russians have a naval base, Port Arthur, in southern Manchuria. But the Tsar does not want to give up all claim to Korea.

Now the Japanese have signed an agreement with Britain. It ensures that Britain will not side with Russia in any future dispute.

CARIBBEAN TOWN VANISHES

May 8, St. Pierre, Martinique   A volcano, Mount Pelée, has erupted and wiped out a whole town. A beautiful lake filling the crater was a favourite spot for French visitors. Last month people complained that there was a terrible smell of sulphur. Today about 28,000 people were overwhelmed by gas fumes and hot steam. Only three people survived. One, a shoemaker, described how he lay in his house, fighting for air. His legs were bleeding, and covered with burns. Another was locked in the only building left standing – the jail.

BOER WAR ENDS

June 1, Vereeniging, Transvaal, South Africa The South African War is over. The Boers have surrendered. Their food is short, many of their horses are dead, and they are exhausted. African tribes have raided their cattle. At midnight last night British and Boer leaders signed a peace treaty. The two Boer republics, the Transvaal, where the new gold mines are, and the Orange Free State, will become British. South Africa is now part of the British Empire.

The news was greeted with great joy by British soldiers, who can now return home. They cheered and fired their guns in salute. The Boer fighters will have to search the camps for their wives and children. Then they will try to rebuild their homes and their lives.

CELEBRATED AUTHOR DIES

Sept 29, Paris The writer Emile Zola died today from carbon monoxide poisoning. The gas came from a charcoal stove in his bedroom. Emile Zola wrote novels about ordinary men and women. Once he spent six months among coal miners so as to write about them truthfully. His novel *The Drunkard* is about the misery of being poor. He was an outspoken socialist. Four years ago he accused a military court of convicting the wrong man in the trial of an army officer, Alfred Dreyfus. The article he wrote caused a scandal, and for a short time he had to leave France.

MINERS' STRIKE ENDS TODAY

Oct 23, Washington The five-month-old strike in the anthracite (coal) mines has led to a shortage of fuel in the United States. President Roosevelt has now reached a settlement with the miners' leader, John Mitchell. Miners' wages will be increased and their working time reduced to nine hours a day. The 150,000 miners were ready to return to work. Without pay their families were starving, and winter is approaching.

The union membership certificate of the United Mine Workers of America

COUNTIES RESPONSIBLE FOR SCHOOLS

Dec 21, London In July Mr. Arthur Balfour succeeded his uncle, Lord Salisbury, as Prime Minister. He has introduced an Act of Parliament by which all schools will be paid for by local councils. The money will come from the rates. Mr. Balfour hopes to raise the standard of schools, most of which are Anglican church schools. Nonconformists have objected. They do not want to pay taxes so that Anglican schools can benefit.

This infants' school is in London.

NEWS IN BRIEF . . .

CHINESE END CRIPPLING CUSTOM

Feb 1, Peking For a thousand years the Chinese have deformed their girl children's feet. They grow up hardly able to walk, with their toes bent under their feet by tight bandaging. In the old days, it was rich women who had to suffer in this way. It showed they did not have to work. Then the villagers copied the fashion. It made their compulsory farmwork extremely painful to perform. Now at last the Emperor has said that this barbaric practice must end.

CHILDREN'S BOOKS SELLING WELL

Oct 2, London Beatrix Potter has just published *The Tale of Peter Rabbit.* Peter, unlike his brothers and sisters, has one aim – to eat the lettuces in Mr McGregor's garden. Mrs. Potter illustrates the story with delicate watercolours. The publishers have already sold 8000 copies.

FASHIONS FLATTER THE FEMALE FIGURE

Aug 1, London This year's fashions are ultra-feminine. Dressmakers and embroiderers are kept busy making up dresses, underslips, petticoats, blouses, skirts, collars and cuffs. Most dresses or blouses have a boned collar that rises to the ears. Tightly laced corsets pull in the waist – to 46 cm (18 inches) for some young women!

Ladies of fashion change their clothes, with the help of a maid, at least three times a day. When they visit friends for a weekend house-party, they naturally take their maids with them.

Fashionable ladies' evening gowns.

IT HAPPENED JUST SO

Dec 1, London Mr. Rudyard Kipling has written *Just So Stories*, fantasy tales about how things came about. They have titles such as 'The Elephant's Child', 'How the Camel got its Hump', and 'The Cat that Walked by Himself'. These stories follow *Kim*, a book about a young boy's adventures in India, where Mr. Kipling was born.

DAM HARNESSES NILE

Dec 10, Egypt As the sluice gates were opened today, a rush of water raced down the River Nile towards Cairo. The huge Aswan Dam, 944 km (590 miles) from the sea, is going to change Egyptian agriculture. In the past an annual flooding has watered the crops. The dam will let water through from the lake above it all the year round.

English and Egyptian guests cross the dam before its opening.

1903

June 12   The Serbian King and Queen are murdered
July 26   Henry Ford markets the Model A car
Sept 30   American sisters reveal plight of the poor
Nov 6   Panama becomes an independent state
Dec 17   The Wright brothers make the first flight

THE TRANSPORT REVOLUTION
FORD MANUFACTURES CHEAP CARS

July 26, Detroit, USA   Mr. Henry Ford has formed a company to make cars that will be both cheap and easy to run. He hopes that his new 'Model A' will sell well. Its top speed is about 48 kph (30 mph).

Two motorists in a 2-cylinder car manufactured by Alexander Wilton have just completed a journey right across America from the Pacific to the Atlantic coasts. It took them only 52 days.

INTERNATIONAL RACE CANCELLED

May 26, Bordeaux, France   The long awaited race from Paris to Madrid in Spain has been called off half-way through. Accidents happened when spectators, unused to high speeds – up to 104 kph (65 mph) – wandered into the road. Six were killed and many more injured.

CARS TO BE CONTROLLED

July 7, London   All private cars in future will be registered. There are now 8500 cars in Britain. Each will display a number, and a letter showing the district where it was registered. The courts will fine anyone found driving dangerously, and sentence drivers to a maximum of three months' imprisonment on the second offence. There will be a speed limit of 16 kph (10 mph) in towns. On the open road the limit is 32 kph (20 mph). Notices will warn drivers of dangerous corners. There are no plans to teach drivers, or to give them tests. Petrol is still a problem: it is often quite difficult to find a shop which supplies it.

AIRSHIP OVER LONDON

Sept 17, London   People walking in the streets saw their first airship today. It flew from Crystal Palace to St. Paul's Cathedral. When the pilot realized that he couldn't go back he landed in a nearby field!

The airship is a huge cigar-shaped balloon filled with gas. Unlike ordinary balloons, it can be steered. Passengers sit in small compartments attached underneath. Three years ago the German inventor, Count Zeppelin, flew the first airship for five kilometres (3½ miles) at about 22 kph (14 mph). This may be a popular method of travel in the future.

Over 200 cars and 59 motorcycles took part in the Paris to Madrid race. This is the first car to reach Bordeaux – in 5 hours, 33 minutes.

HEAVIER-THAN-AIR MACHINE TAKES OFF

Dec 17, Kitty Hawk, USA The Wright brothers, Orville and Wilbur, have proved that man can fly. Unlike a lighter-than-air balloon, their machine has wings. Today Mr. Orville Wright flew their home-made machine, the *Flyer*, for 59 seconds – almost a minute! The 13 horsepower engine drives two wooden propellers with the aid of toughened bicycle chains. There are two wings, and Mr. Wright lies on the bottom one. He controls the machine by moving his feet and hands.

Just nine days ago a distinguished scientist, Mr. Samuel Langley, also launched a home-made machine from a houseboat. It plunged straight into the river.

Though the successful *Flyer* ended its flight in a nose-dive, this is seen as the beginning of great things for the Wright brothers – and perhaps for the world.

At Kitty Hawk in North Carolina, the Wright Brothers, Orville and Wilbur, fly their machine for the first time.

POVERTY IN BRITAIN AND AMERICA

HOUSING FOR THE POOR

April 27, London The Prince of Wales has laid the foundation stone of a block of workers' cottages in Westminster. The Prince is very concerned about social conditions. Hundreds of men who volunteered to fight in the Boer War had to be turned away: they were too badly fed to make good soldiers. About 30 per cent of Britons live on the edge of starvation. Most work eleven or twelve hours each day; if they are lucky they take home £1 a week. And 'home' may be one or two rooms, with no running water, and a shared lavatory out in the open. About 250,000 people are so poor they have to live in the workhouses. Yet Britain is the richest nation in the world.

This London family live in one room, with no tap.

PLIGHT OF WORKERS REVEALED

Sept 30, New York Two sisters, Marie and Bessie Van Vorst, have spent the past few months dressed as poor working women. They found out what conditions are like in factories and 'sweat shops'. They saw small children of about 8 or 10 years old working for 25 cents a day. There are over a million workers under 16. Women doing piece-work at home earn less than a dollar for 14 hours' work. Many are underfed and suffer from tuberculosis. Garment workers, mainly Polish women, are fortunate in having their own trade union.

KING VISITS FRANCE

May 1, Paris King Edward VII's visit to France began this morning. He is here on a goodwill mission. The French have been suspicious of the British for some years. They took the side of the Boers in the South African war. The government hopes the King's 'common touch' will help to convince them of Britain's friendship.

King Edward VII visits the Paris Opera.

SERBIAN KING MURDERED

June 12, Belgrade Army officers yesterday broke into the royal palace and murdered King Alexander and Queen Droga. The King was hated because of his one-man rule. He did away with the constitution in April, and dismissed ten judges. Newspapers today, free from censorship at last, say the rebels 'rendered a tremendous service'. In Turkey, where newspapers have no freedom, the royal couple are said to have died of indigestion.

PANAMA IS INDEPENDENT STATE

Nov 6, Washington Panama has revolted against rule from the South American state of Colombia. Cut off from Panama by jungle and high ground, the Colombians approached by sea to put down the revolt. They briefly bombarded Panama City, killing one man and one donkey. The Americans are hoping to build a canal across the narrow neck of land that joins North and South America. It will run through Panama. Two days ago they landed marines at Colón on the coast, and the Colombians departed without a fight.

WOMAN SHARES NOBEL PRIZE

Dec 10, Stockholm Madame Marie Curie is the first woman ever to win a Nobel Prize. She has been given this honour jointly with her husband, Pierre, and Monsieur Henri Becquerel. The three scientists have all done original work in what Madame Curie has called 'radioactivity'. She has shown that a new substance, called radium, sends out heat without chemical change. Two other substances discovered by the Curies, uranium and thorium, are also 'radioactive'.

Marie Curie and her husband Pierre

NEWS IN BRIEF . . .

BLIND GIRL'S STORY TOLD

Mar 31, New York *The Story of My Life*, by Helen Keller, has become an instant success. Miss Keller became blind and deaf as a child, but despite this she enjoys life to the full. Mr. Mark Twain, who wrote stories about Tom Sawyer and Huckleberry Finn, is one of her friends.

Helen Keller (left) and her teacher

NEW POPE CROWNED

Aug 9, Rome Pope Pius X was crowned today in St. Peter's Church, Rome. The elaborate and colourful ceremony, which lasted five hours, was watched by 70,000 people. The previous pope, Leo XIII, died three weeks ago aged 93.

BICYCLE RACE IS A TOUGH RIDE

July 19, Paris The first bicycle race, which its inventor, Henry Desgrange, calls the 'Tour de France', ended today. A 32-year-old chimney-sweep, Maurice Garin, crossed the finishing line after 94½ hours' cycling time. The next competitor did not arrive till three hours later. The 4000-km (2485-mile) route took the cyclists right down to Marseilles and back to Paris. For 17 days they cycled: they signed in at ten different places and there was a time limit for each of these stages. Mr. Garin says he rode late into the night to reach his targets in time. Out of 60 starters, 21 riders finished the gruelling course.

The new pope, Pius X, in Rome

PILGRIMS PUT PAID TO PIRATES

Oct 13, New York The new baseball competition, to be called the World Series, has finally had its first triumph. For months baseball fans have been waiting for the most exciting game ever held by the American League. And today, after 12 days' play, the Boston Pilgrims defeated the Pittsburgh Pirates by 5 games to 3. The League hopes that this battle of the giants of baseball will occur yearly in future.

CONTROVERSIAL ARTIST DIES

July 17, Chelsea, London The American-born painter, James Whistler, died today aged 70. The critics did not like his pictures; Whistler sued his chief critic, John Ruskin, for writing insulting remarks. He won the court case, but was awarded only a farthing [a quarter of a penny] in damages. However, the publicity did him good. At an exhibition he wrote the critics' remarks under each picture. The public did not agree with the critics, and his work began to sell.

Whistler's *Nocturne in blue and gold*

BRUTALITY PUNISHED IN NORTH GERMANY

Dec 15, Rensburg, Germany Lieut. Bilse has written a book about conditions in the German army. He says that in Prussian regiments soldiers are frequently beaten almost to death. Several soldiers have committed suicide after being punished. In August an officer was found guilty of 576 incidents of brutality and imprisoned for two and a half years.

1904

Jan 9	Somali dervishes face British troops
May 30	Russians are besieged in Manchuria
Sept 7	British and Tibetans sign treaty
Nov 7	Captain Scott speaks of polar expedition

CONFLICT IN FAR EAST
JAPAN AND RUSSIA ARE AT WAR

Feb 10, Manchuria   The Russians have been moving troops into Korea to defend it against Japan. Tsar Nicholas II thought that Japan would not dare to go to war with his huge country. He was wrong. Two days ago, at midnight, the Japanese torpedoed Russian warships at their naval base in Port Arthur, Manchuria. Their warships are now surrounding the harbour, and they have declared war on Russia. Russia cannot afford to fight a war, particularly one so far from home. It will take time for more troops to arrive in Port Arthur because the one-track Trans-Siberian Railway is not completed. Meanwhile, well-equipped Japanese troops are landing in Korea.

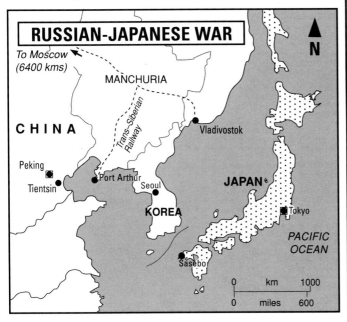

RUSSIAN-JAPANESE WAR

PORT ARTHUR IS BESIEGED

May 30, Manchuria   The Japanese and Russians have fought a bitter battle near Port Arthur. The Russian General Stössel ordered his troops to retreat. They are now besieged in Port Arthur by the Japanese land and sea forces.

RUSSIAN FLEET BADLY DAMAGED

Aug 31, Manchuria   The Russian flagship has limped into Port Arthur. It is badly damaged, and the fleet commander, Admiral Witgeft, has been killed. The Admiral had led his fleet out of the harbour secretly. He was trying to make a dash for Vladivostok, but he encountered the Japanese navy. Both sides tried to wreck the other's flagship. Admiral Witgeft and his officers were killed by shells, and the signalling equipment was destroyed. It took some time before the second-in-command, in another battleship, realized this. When he did, he signalled the fleet to retreat.

HORROR OF UNEXPLAINED SHELLING

Oct 24, Hull   Three days ago Russian warships shelled British fishing vessels off the Dogger Bank in the North Sea. One trawler was sunk and others badly damaged. The Russian fleet, on its way to the East, sailed on to Port Arthur without stopping. The Russian warships apparently thought the trawlers were Japanese warships. This incident has turned the British public against Russia. Ships of the Royal Navy are sailing to the Dogger Bank to prevent further incidents.

DERVISHES FLEE FROM BATTLEFIELD

Jan 9, British Somaliland   Trouble has been brewing in this East African colony. A Muslim leader, Sayyid Muhammad Hasan, has for several years been fighting the British in a guerrilla war. He calls his followers 'dervishes'. They call him the Poor Man of God, but to the British he is 'the Mad Mullah'. (A mullah is a holy man in Islam.) Today the dervishes encountered the British forces in an open plain, with no tree or hill cover. Seven thousand dervishes, fighting on horseback with pistols and knives, were killed by British long-range cannons. The mullah and his remaining forces fled to the east. They will no doubt fight again another day.

British soldiers receive news of the mullah.

EXPEDITION REACHES LLASA

Sept 7, Llasa, Tibet   British and Tibetan representatives have signed a trade treaty. This is the end of a strange and sad story. The British viceroy in India thought the Russians were trying to control Tibet. He persuaded the British government to send Colonel Francis Younghusband, the explorer, into Tibet to investigate. He took a thousand soldiers, Indian carriers, and pack animals.

On the way to Llasa the army nearly froze to death, and many soldiers suffered from frostbite and snow-blindness. When they arrived in Llasa after eight months they found no sign of any Russians. The British troops had killed over 2000 Tibetans, many of them unarmed. The expedition's hardships were a high price to pay for an agreement to trade with Tibet, which, in any case, has very little to sell.

STRANGE EVENTS AT OLYMPICS

Aug 29, St. Louis, Missouri   American competitors won most of the medals in this year's Olympics, held during the United States World Fair. The marathon attracted much attention. Fred Lorz (US) arrived at the finishing post well ahead of the rest, and not at all out of breath. But he was disqualified. He admitted that he rode on a lorry for part of the way!

FRENCH AND BRITISH AGREE

April 8, London   French people booed King Edward VII when he visited France last year. They now cheer him whenever he appears in public. Today an *entente cordiale*, or friendly understanding, was signed by French and British delegates. The French have agreed to leave Egypt, which they have been ruling jointly with Britain. In return they expect Britain to give them a mandate over Morocco, if the Sultan's rule should break down.

The Sultan has very little control over Morocco. Berber tribesmen have seized the capital, Fez. They are led by a man named Bu Hamara ('The Man with a Donkey'), who accuses the Sultan of following Western ways.

Ships of the French fleet at Portsmouth

SCOTT EXPLORES SOUTH

Nov 7, London Tonight at the Albert Hall Captain Robert Falcon Scott spoke of his expedition to the South Polar regions. During the past three years his ship, *Discovery*, has been home to scientists collecting information about the flora and fauna of these barren lands. Captain Scott has led explorers far out onto the ice towards the South Pole.

'SQUARE DEAL' PRESIDENT WINS

Nov 9, Washington Theodore Roosevelt has been re-elected President of the United States. His motto is 'Speak softly and carry a big stick'. This is how he hopes to conduct his foreign policy: courteously but firmly. His campaign supporters wore a badge that promised 'A square deal for all'.

Scott's ship *Discovery* abandoned in frozen Antarctic seas. From April to July each year the sun never rose above the horizon. When food ran out, the explorers lived on seal and dog meat.

NEWS IN BRIEF . . .

OUTDOOR SMOKING? MEN ONLY!

Sept 28, New York Today a vigilant policeman arrested a young lady as she sat in her car on New York's fashionable Fifth Avenue. What had she done? Nothing illegal; but she was smoking a cigarette in full view of people passing by. The tobacco industry, through advertising, encourages every adult to smoke cigarettes. But the police seem to think that ladies should smoke only in private.

SHAW FEATURES SALVATION ARMY

Nov 1, London In Mr. George Bernard Shaw's new play, *Major Barbara*, an arms manufacturer's daughter joins the Salvation Army to help her father's workers. Women in Mr. Shaw's plays are often strong characters, and this one is no exception. In March he astonished theatregoers with *John Bull's Other Island*, a play about Ireland. The Prime Minister has seen it several times, and at a command performance the King laughed so much he broke his chair.

Mr. George Bernard Shaw, the playwright

1905

Jan 22   Troops massacre Russian demonstrators
Mar 31   German Kaiser visits Morocco
May 27   Japanese defeat Russians in Tsushima straits
Oct 14   Women demonstrate for the right to vote

RUSSIA'S ENEMIES AT HOME AND ABROAD

UNARMED WORKERS MASSACRED

Jan 22, St Petersburg   Many hundreds of unarmed demonstrators, men, women and children, were killed today and thousands more were wounded in the square outside the Tsar's Winter Palace. A young church leader, Father George Gapon, led a peaceful demonstration to protest to the Tsar about working conditions, and against the war with Japan. The people's message was 'Destroy the wall between yourself and your people', for they believe that the Tsar is not told about working conditions by his ministers. They chanted 'God Save the Tsar'. But the Tsar had fled. Police and soldiers were called out, and they fired into the crowd of about 200,000 people. Tonight the square is full of the dead and the injured.

Troops attack the crowd of men, women and children at the Winter Palace in St. Petersburg.

RUSSIA LOSES BATTLE IN MANCHURIA

March 10, Manchuria   Port Arthur fell to the Japanese in January. For the past two weeks the Russians have been hard pressed near the Manchurian town of Mukden. Each side has lost about 60,000 men. In spite of successful charges by the Cossacks, Russia's cavalry, the Russians have now had to give in to the nation they call 'The Yellow Peril'. The Russian general has resigned.

The Russians are now relying on their navy. A fleet of battleships left the Baltic Sea in November. They have to sail half way round the world: west of Africa and across the Indian Ocean.

RUSSIAN FLEET DESTROYED

May 27, Japan   Today Japanese warships caught the Russian fleet in the narrow waters between Japan and Korea, the Tsushima Straits. In a battle lasting 24 hours, the Japanese Admiral Togo scored a great victory. His ships surrounded the Russian fleet and sunk or damaged most of its ships. Nearly 5000 Russian sailors have been killed. It is the first time in history that an Asian country has defeated a European one.

RUSSIAN DISCONTENT OVER DEFEAT

June 27, St. Petersburg News of the disaster at Tsushima has reached the Russian capital. People are angry with the Tsar's handling of the war. The crew of the battleship *Potemkin* has mutinied, thrown the officers overboard, and sailed the ship to Odessa. Here sympathizers have been fighting in the streets, and several thousand people have been killed in the disturbances.

The Russian battleship *Potemkin*

TSAR APPOINTS PRIME MINISTER

Oct 17, St. Petersburg With two million people on strike and industry at a standstill, the Tsar has at last agreed that in future he will not rule alone. He has appointed a parliament, the Duma, with a Prime Minister, Count Witte. Members of the new Socialist parties are afraid that the Tsar and his successors will still have too much power. His chief critic is a leader of the Workers' Soviet (council) in St. Petersburg, Leo Trotsky.

KAISER VISITS MOROCCO

March 31, Tangier Last year Britain agreed that France should have a mandate over Morocco. The Germans feel that they have been left out. The German Kaiser has arrived on a visit to Morocco. He rode through the streets of this port on a magnificent Berber horse. He told the Moroccan Sultan, Abdul Aziz, that all European nations should be equal trading partners with Morocco. The French are not likely to be pleased.

FASHION-CONSCIOUS AT THE DERBY

May 31, Epsom A huge crowd watched Cicero win the Derby this afternoon. The enclosure was full of top-hatted gentlemen. Top hats are always worn for the Derby. For Newmarket races the fashion-conscious wear bowler hats, as approved by the King. Following his lead, men attending afternoon engagements wear trousers, a short jacket and a top hat. For evening parties they wear knee-breeches, not trousers – but on board a yacht it is the other way round! The King is often seen wearing a close-fitting overcoat, and a large gold pin holds his tie in place. In his favourite holiday resort, Biarritz in France, he wears a more informal blue jacket with white trousers. The King can be very annoyed with friends who do not keep his fashion rules.

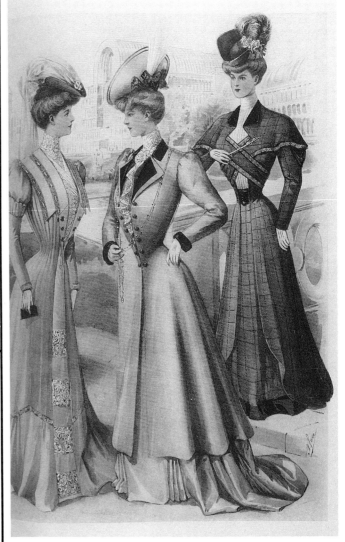

These costumes are what today's ladies of fashion wear to the races.

RUSSIANS AND GERMANS IN ALLIANCE

July 20, Baltic Sea The Kaiser today met the Russian Tsar on board a ship off the Baltic coast, and they agreed on an alliance. After his country's defeat in Japan, the Tsar is happy to unite with a strong country. The desire for 'spheres of influence' as countries take sides in international disputes could easily lead to war on a grand scale.

The Tsar (left) welcomes the German Kaiser aboard his yacht.

WOMEN WANT THE VOTE

Oct 20, Manchester Today hundreds of angry women gathered here. These 'suffragettes' say that women should be allowed to vote for Members of Parliament, as men do. Two of their leaders, Miss Christabel Pankhurst and Miss Annie Kenney, were arrested yesterday. At the Liberal Party's election meeting, Miss Kenney challenged the Liberal leader and called him a coward. Outside, there was a scuffle with the police, who arrested the two women. Only in Australia and New Zealand do women have the vote.

Miss Pankhurst and Miss Kenney (centre) are guests of honour at a Manchester meeting.

NEWS IN BRIEF . . .

PIMPERNEL RESCUES FRENCH PRISONERS

July 31, London The adventure story, *The Scarlet Pimpernel*, was published earlier this year. It has had a stunning success. The hero is Sir Percy Blakeney, a British lord. He slips into France in disguise to rescue prisoners of the French Revolution. Many are saved from the guillotine by Sir Percy – yet nobody, not even his wife, knows that he is the 'Scarlet Pimpernel'.

The author, Baroness Orczy, says the idea came to her while she was waiting for an underground train.

MAGIC AT THE NICKLEODEON

April 5, New York Enterprising businessmen have begun to entertain audiences with a new kind of show. They have rented about 300 old warehouses or stores in the city, and filled them with seats and a piano. Having paid a nickel (5 cents) entrance fee, you can be entertained by pictures which actually move as you watch. The audience can see, flickering across a white screen, moving pictures of dancers, mock fights, and slapstick comedy.

Meanwhile a pianist plays suitable music. One message often appears on the screen. It reads: 'Will the ladies please remove their hats.'

THE GREAT MAN IS ALIVE

March 31, London Sherlock Holmes is back! In the last story about the great detective, he and his enemy, Dr. Moriarty, disappeared over a cliff in Switzerland. His inventor, Sir Arthur Conan Doyle, was tired of him! But now, by popular demand, he and his friend Dr. Watson are detecting again, in *The Return of Sherlock Holmes*.

Holmes stories are printed in the *Strand Magazine*. The magazine does not print serial stories, so Sir Arthur decided to write a series of different adventures, all about Holmes. This had not been tried before. People love them so much that they think of Sherlock Holmes as a real person.

1906

Feb 10	HMS *Dreadnought* is launched
Mar 30	French miners are rescued
April 8	Mount Vesuvius erupts
April 19	San Francisco is destroyed by earthquake
July 21	Major Dreyfus becomes a hero in France

SUPER BATTLESHIP LAUNCHED

Feb 10, Plymouth Britain has launched a battleship of a new improved type. HMS *Dreadnought* has ten 12-inch guns, which can swing round to fire in any direction. Though the British navy has not been in serious action since 1805, Admiral Fisher warns that Britain should still 'rule the waves'. He plans to build new 'battle-cruisers', which will be swift and well armed.

The British Admiralty has studied Admiral Togo's ships and tactics at the Battle of Tsushima. They approve his decision not to use submarines, which one admiral has called 'underhand and unfair'. In spite of Mr. Marconi's invention of the wireless, all navies still use flags for signalling.

The super-battleship HMS *Dreadnought* in a painting by Norman Wilkinson

LIBERALS FORM NEW PARLIAMENT

Feb 7, London The Liberals today won a great victory in the general election. The Education Act of 1902, and the question of tariff reform have turned the country against the Conservatives. The new Prime Minister is Sir Henry Campbell-Bannerman.

Mr. James Keir Hardie, MP for Merthyr in Wales, has started a new political party, the Labour Party. Most members of the party are trade unionists.

AFRICAN RISING PUT DOWN

Feb 27, Songea, Tanganyika Africans in this German colony are rebelling against foreign rule. It is called the Maji Maji Rising. A 'prophet' named Kinjikitile supplied people with *maji* (medicine) which he said would turn European bullets to water. Hundreds of Africans stormed a government outpost, where they were killed by machine-guns. A shocked African said: "They were severely beaten as the machine-gun helped the Germans very much. They fought up to five in the evening. When they realized they were being killed in numbers, they fled, crying, 'Kinjikitile, you have cheated us'." Similar incidents occurred all over the country. The situation is now under control; a number of African leaders have been hanged.

Africans work long hours on European plantations, cultivating crops for export. They have little time to tend their own fields, on which they depend for their food. As in other European-owned African countries, the Africans have no say in the government.

VIOLENT EARTH SHOCKS CAUSE DAMAGE

VOLCANO BLOWS ITS TOP

April 8, Naples, Italy The top of Mount Vesuvius in southern Italy has been blown off by a violent eruption. Onlookers saw a huge cloud 'like a pine tree', and vivid lightning flashes as lava poured down the mountainside. A town has been destroyed, villages are half buried, and 105 people died when a church roof collapsed.

EARTHQUAKE DESTROYS CITY

April 19, San Francisco Yesterday a tremendous earthquake destroyed this Californian town. Starting at dawn, a series of shocks tore up roads and split buildings in two. Fires, caused by broken gas mains, have destroyed more property than the earthquake itself. Firemen were powerless, as the town's water mains were out of action. Thieves trying to loot shops have been shot by police and soldiers. It is one of the worst earthquakes ever recorded. Over a thousand people have died, and about 250,000 have been left homeless.

Sacramento Street in San Francisco after the earthquake devastated the city

NEW QUAKE IN SOUTH AMERICA

Aug 18, Chile Valparaiso and Santiago have been partially destroyed by an earthquake that has left hundreds dead. About 40 villages and towns also suffered heavy damage. The earthquake followed a night of pouring rain.

TYPHOON HITS HONG KONG

Sept 18, Hong Kong Winds and heavy rain raged today for two hours. Several large ships were driven onto the shore, and hundreds of fishing boats were sunk. There are 10,000 people dead or missing.

MOROCCO TO BE FRENCH MANDATE

March 31, Algeciras, Spain An international conference on North Africa has just ended after two months. The delegates finally agreed that France should have a mandate over Morocco. This means that France will protect the country, and have certain trading rights there. The Sultan will still rule the country, under Muslim laws. Spain holds some ports, and the south-western part of the country.

France now has a great bloc of West and North-West Africa under her control. European nations have successfully partitioned Africa between them. Only Ethiopia and Liberia remain independent.

VIOLENT INCIDENT IN EGYPT

June 27, Denshawai, Egypt On June 13, British officers went to shoot pigeons near this village. The villagers keep the pigeons in special brick houses, and they protested at the shooting. In the uproar three men and a woman were shot. A British officer died of concussion, and an Egyptian who tried to help him was killed by a second British officer.

The British administration in Egypt has sentenced the headman and three other villagers to death, and two to prison for life. Others received 50 lashes. Egyptians are shocked at this unfair treatment. The English officer who killed an Egyptian was not punished at all.

NEWS IN BRIEF . . .

TRAPPED MINERS RESCUED

March 30, Courrières, Pas de Calais After 20 days underground, 13 miners have been brought to the surface alive. A huge explosion at daybreak on March 10 wrecked the lifts which carry miners underground. Altogether, 1800 miners were either in the lifts or already underground, and 1787 died.

Government officials at the mine.

PRESIDENT HONOURED

Dec 10, Stockholm President Roosevelt has won the Nobel Peace Prize, because he persuaded Russia and Japan to end their war. The peace treaty was signed in September at Portsmouth, New Hampshire. Roosevelt is the first American to be honoured in this way.

Dreyfus receives the Legion of Honour.

ANTI-JEWISH RIOTS

June 15, St. Petersburg The Russian Duma was asked today whether it is trying to stop offences against Jews. Yesterday peasant mobs attacked a Jewish quarter and killed several hundred people. The peasants claimed that the Jews fired on a religious procession, when two priests and several children were killed. The police took the side of the peasants, and distributed leaflets saying Jews should be wiped out.

ARMY OFFICER HONOURED

July 21, Paris Everyone in France has heard of Major Alfred Dreyfus, and taken sides for or against him. In 1895 he denied spying. But he was found guilty and imprisoned on Devil's Island, in French Guiana, the maximum security prison.

Major Dreyfus was pardoned six years ago, but his innocence was not proved. Since then the real culprit has been found. Today Major Dreyfus received the Legion of Honour.

1907

Mar 22   Indians resist South African law
July 28   'Big Bill' Haywood acquitted of murder
Oct 31   US fleet sails round the world
Nov 28   Belgium government to buy Congo from King
Nov 29   Florence Nightingale receives the Order of Merit

CONGO CHANGES HANDS
AFRICANS' SUFFERING REVEALED

May 1, London   The British public is shocked by reports from the Congo Free State. The Belgian King, Leopold II, personally owns this Central African territory, which is 80 times the size of Belgium. He has become rich from the sale of its wild rubber (from forest trees, not plantations) and its ivory.

Mr. Roger Casement, the British consul in the Congo, reported on conditions there in 1904. Africans have to pay taxes to Belgium. As they have no currency, they pay not in money, but in wild rubber. To get enough rubber, they work long hours, deep in the forests. If they do not collect enough, they are punished. Some are brutally beaten, others have their hands cut off.

LORDS DEBATE CONGO SITUATION

July 29, London   Today the House of Lords heard about conditions in the Congo Free State. It was reported that the population there has fallen by 3 million in only 15 years. Much of this is due to a terrible epidemic of sleeping-sickness, the disease caused by the bite of the tsetse fly. Survivors are too weak to harvest the wild rubber. Thousands of villagers have died from exhaustion, starvation or disease. Thousands more have been shot. The elephant herds have dwindled. The wild rubber trees have all been tapped, and nobody has planted any more.

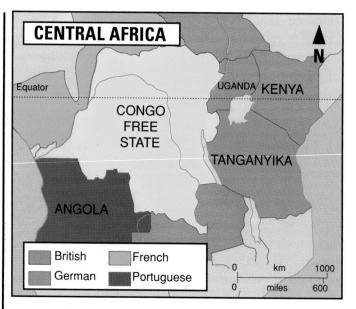

CENTRAL AFRICA

N

Equator — UGANDA / KENYA

CONGO FREE STATE

TANGANYIKA

ANGOLA

| British | French |
| German | Portuguese |

0 — km — 1000
0 — miles — 600

BELGIAN GOVERNMENT BUYS CONGO

Nov 28, Brussels   The Belgian government is going to buy the Congo Free State from the King. This has been decided after much debate in the Belgian parliament. The Belgian people did not know that the King's agents were mistreating the Africans and managing the country so badly.

SOUTH AFRICAN RACE LAW RESISTED

March 22, Pretoria   A new law in the Transvaal state of South Africa has angered Indians. In future they will be finger-printed, and will have to carry identity cards. Their leader, Mr. Mohandas Gandhi, is calling for people to resist the new law by peaceful means. Mr. Gandhi was born in north-western India. He trained as a lawyer in England, and has been a lawyer in South Africa for 14 years.

AUTHOR BACKS FARMERS

May 8, Norfolk Mr. Rider Haggard is famous for his African adventure stories, such as *King Solomon's Mines*. His campaign to improve Britain's countryside is less well known. He has travelled all over England, and says that the country's farming is in a bad way. Farm prices are low. Many country dwellers have moved to the towns. Forests have been cut down and no trees planted to replace them. There is soil erosion and neglect. He would like to see boys educated on farms in the summer, and go to school in winter. He wants the government to grant loans for the purchase of farms and smallholdings. The government says it will investigate his idea.

WORKERS WAGE WINE WAR

June 20, Narbonne, France Police fired on demonstrators today as the 'wine war' enters its second month. Wine growers are protesting at low prices. Although Prime Minister Georges Clemenceau backs social reform, he deals harshly with strikers. Last month he called in the troops when strikers burnt the town hall and police station in another wine-growing town.

Vineyard workers riot in the Champagne district.

'WOBBLIES' LEADER ACQUITTED OF MURDER

July 28, Idaho, USA Mr. Clarence Darrow, the brilliant young Chicago lawyer, has been defending 'Big Bill' Haywood in a murder trial. When Frank Steunenberg, former governor of Idaho, was murdered by dynamite, Haywood and his colleague, Harry Orchard, were arrested. Orchard has admitted that he planted the bomb. There is no evidence against Haywood, though he is known to favour violence. He started the Industrial Workers of the World (known as the Wobblies) two years ago. Their aim is to overthrow capitalism. Mr. Darrow has persuaded the jury to acquit Haywood.

PUBLIC WITHDRAWS MONEY FROM BANKS

Nov 4, New York Businessmen in the United States all invest in stocks and shares. There are even special share offices for ladies. The economy has been booming for ten years. Recently an investor's gamble on the Stock Exchange failed, and the bank backing him lost heavily. Bank customers were afraid that the bank would collapse, and rushed to take out their money. Soon customers were closing their accounts with other banks. Fortunately Mr. John Pierpont Morgan, head of the US Steel Corporation, has persuaded bankers to put in 25 million dollars to save the banks. He is said to have locked them into his library until they agreed!

NEWS IN BRIEF . . .

BOYS INVITED TO BECOME SCOUTS

July 29, London Sir Robert Baden-Powell has started a movement for boys which he calls the Boy Scouts. He was impressed by the competence of boy soldiers at Mafeking. He believes that training in tracking, climbing, basic survival techniques, and a wide range of other outdoor activities will help young men to grow up honestly and fearlessly. The Scouts will wear a uniform, and will have organized meetings and summer camps.

Lord Robert Baden-Powell

TAXI! TAXI!

May 31, New York The first taxi-cabs to run on meters – 65 of them – have been seen in New York streets. The bright red motors have been imported from France. Policemen now have new duties, to direct traffic in busy towns.

ARTIST PAINTED IN NEW STYLE

Oct 15, Paris An exhibition of 60 paintings by the French artist Paul Cézanne here in Paris is revealing the artist's remarkable control of blocks of colour. He sees the shapes of nature in terms of cylinders, spheres and squares. He seems to have changed the art of painting – a change which the Spanish artist Pablo Picasso is continuing. Cézanne was still hard at work painting when he died last year.

GREAT WHITE FLEET SAILS

Oct 31, Japan President Roosevelt of the USA has sent a fleet of 16 battleships to sail around the world. They are painted white. This 'goodwill cruise' is also meant to show the strength of America's navy. The President was not sure if the fleet would be welcome in Japan. Japanese immigration into the United States has recently been restricted. It follows a row that broke out when California set up separate schools for Asian children. This has now been altered.

Though many Japanese who wished to emigrate to America are dismayed, the crowd gave the American sailors a great welcome. On its return, the fleet will have sailed 73,600 km (46,000 miles) altogether.

KING'S EXPENSIVE PRESENT

Nov 9, Sandringham, Norfolk Today, on the King's 66th birthday, the South African government gave him the largest diamond in the world. It was mined two years ago at Kimberley in South Africa, and it weighs 0.6 kg (1¼ lb). It is called the Cullinan diamond. It will be sent to an Amsterdam diamond dealer, who will cut it into nine separate stones. The King wants the largest ones to be set in the royal crown and sceptre.

WAR-TIME NURSE HONOURED

Nov 29, London Miss Florence Nightingale has been granted the Order of Merit by the King. She is the first woman to receive this honour. Only 24 people are entitled to put 'OM' after their names at any one time.

During the Crimean War, in 1854, Miss Nightingale ran a hospital for wounded soldiers in Russia. She raised the standard of care so that far fewer men died from septic wounds. Thousands owe their lives to the nurse they called 'The Lady with the Lamp'.

Florence Nightingale, centre, honoured today with the Order of Merit

1908

April 12	Asquith becomes Prime Minister
Oct 3	Unemployed take part in London 'hunger march'
Oct 6	Bulgaria leaves the Turkish Empire
Dec 22	Suffragettes are released from jail
Dec 29	Sicilian town destroyed by earthquake

TURKISH PARTY OPPOSES SULTAN
TURKISH GENERAL ASSASSINATED

July 7, Monastir, Macedonia A Turkish General has today been shot dead in the streets of Monastir. He was sent by the Sultan of Turkey, Abdul Hamid II, to put down a mutiny in the Turkish army. The rebellious soldiers have joined the 'Young Turk' movement. The Young Turks are not necessarily young, but belong to a political party of this name which opposes the Sultan. The party believes he is ruining their country, which was once the centre of the great Ottoman empire.

Last month the British King and the Russian Tsar discussed self-rule for Macedonia, which is a Turkish possession. The Young Turks are afraid the Sultan will agree to give up Macedonia. The Turkish empire has already lost many of its former colonies because of the Sultan's weakness.

SULTAN MUST APPOINT PARLIAMENT

July 24, Constantinople After pressure from the Young Turks, the Sultan has agreed that Turkey should have a constitution and a parliament. Even the words 'constitution' and 'parliament' have been banned from newspapers for many years for fear of what the ordinary people would demand. The Sultan has always opposed change. The Young Turks hope that free discussion in a parliament will help Turkey develop new ideas, and to take its place in the world as a modern nation, rather than as a country always looking to the past.

ANCIENT PALACE FOUND

Aug 27, Crete The archaeologist Sir Arthur Evans is excavating a huge forgotten palace on the island of Crete. He has found hundreds of stone tablets, all with unreadable characters in Greek script. They are 3000 years old. A remarkable wall-painting shows a girl acrobat leaping over a bull. Thousands of years ago the Greek poet Homer wrote: "there is Knossos, the great city, the place where Minos was king". Sir Arthur believes he has found Knossos, King Minos's capital city. He is calling this ancient civilization 'Minoan'.

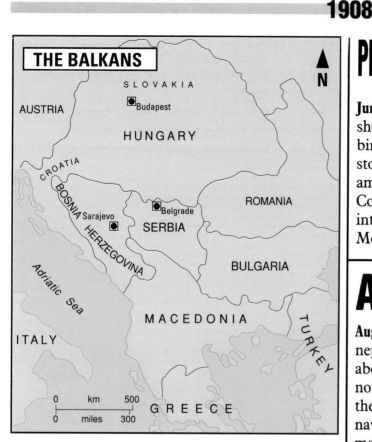

THE BALKANS

SLOVAKIA

AUSTRIA · Budapest

HUNGARY

CROATIA

BOSNIA HERZEGOVINA · Sarajevo

Belgrade

SERBIA

ROMANIA

BULGARIA

Adriatic Sea

ITALY

MACEDONIA

TURKEY

GREECE

0 km 500
0 miles 300

CRISIS IN THE BALKANS

Oct 6, Belgrade, Serbia Two surprise moves have angered the Serbians and alerted western nations. Yesterday Bulgaria proclaimed its independence from the Turkish empire, and today the Austrians took Bosnia-Herzegovina, also from the Turks.

Serbia has always wanted to join up with Bosnia, once a Serbian territory. The Serbians are now talking of war with Austria, which has the support of Germany. Once again European nations are taking sides and forming alliances.

KING MEETS NEW PRIME MINISTER

April 12, Biarritz, France Sir Henry Campbell-Bannerman has resigned as Prime Minister because of illness. Today the new Prime Minister, Mr. Herbert Asquith, travelled by train across France to meet the King, who is on holiday in Biarritz. The change of leadership has brought alterations in the Liberal government. Mr. David Lloyd George is the new Chancellor of the Exchequer, and Mr. Winston Churchill will lead the important Ministry of Trade.

PRESIDENT CALLS FOR NATIONAL PARKS

June 8, Washington President Roosevelt has been shocked by forest felling, and the shooting of rare birds and animals. Souvenir hunters shatter the stone of Arizona's petrified forest to look for amethysts. Today he has called for a National Conservation Commission. Areas of outstanding interest will become National Parks and National Monuments.

ARMING FOR WAR?

Aug 11, Germany King Edward VII has met his nephew, the German Kaiser Wilhelm II, to talk about their 'spheres of influence'. The two men do not get on very well, but everyone hopes this time they can agree. The arms race is alarming. The navies of both countries are building more and more battleships. The Germans count on their zeppelins to control the skies.

Wilhelm II, the German Kaiser

GIVE US JOBS, SAY WORKLESS

Oct 3, London A crowd of unemployed men gathered in Trafalgar Square today. They have taken part in a 'hunger march'. Last month a similar crowd gathered in Glasgow. With banners and placards they are trying to gain the public's attention. There are nearly a million hungry people in the British Isles.

Mrs. Emmeline and Miss Christabel Pankhurst

PANKHURSTS RELEASED FROM JAIL

Dec 22, London   Women who attended a suffragette meeting today welcomed with cheers their leader, Mrs. Emmeline Pankhurst, and her daughter Miss Christabel Pankhurst. Both women have spent two months in jail. They have had to wear badly fitting prison clothes and boots, and have been kept in total silence. But in spite of this ordeal, they are determined to continue with their campaign. If women are not allowed to vote, they argue, they are just second-class citizens.

OLYMPICS END TODAY

Oct 31, White City, London   A huge new stadium was built at White City for the Olympic Games. In spite of bad weather, a large crowd turned out to see 21 different sports, including rowing (at Henley) and tennis (at Wimbledon). Three American runners seemed to block the way for a British runner in the 400 metres. Americans refused a re-run, so the British runner was given an unexpected win.

The marathon winner was disqualified for being helped over the line! He was given an unofficial prize.

SICILIAN TOWN DESTROYED

Dec 29, Messina, Italy The worst earthquake ever recorded in Europe, and a huge tidal wave, yesterday hit Messina, a port on the east coast of Sicily. It is estimated that 84,000 people died here, and across the straits on the 'toe' of Italy. The Sicilian shoreline sank by half a metre overnight. Most of the houses and shops, the 900-year-old Norman cathedral and many beautiful churches have been totally destroyed.

The port of Messina in ruins and in flames after the earthquake

NEWS IN BRIEF . . .

PROTEST LEADER JAILED

Jan 10, Pretoria, South Africa Mr. Gandhi, leader of the Indian community here, has been jailed for two months. Thousands of Indians have left the province because they refuse to carry identity cards. Many are traders, and their absence is hitting the economy.

AIRSHIP TOTALLY DESTROYED

Aug 5, Germany A zeppelin went up in flames today after it had been hit by lightning. Several passengers were injured. The airship was on the ground at the time, refuelling its 16 gas tanks with hydrogen. It was returning after a test flight to Lake Constance, where it is moored.

FISHING TOWN ELECTS NEW MAYOR

Nov 9, Aldeburgh, Suffolk Dr. Elizabeth Garrett Anderson has become Britain's first woman mayor. She became the first woman doctor in Britain 35 years ago. Medicine was a man's profession in those days, and she had to fight to be admitted to the university course. She did so well that not only did she get a British degree, but the University of Paris gave her one too.

PROFESSOR SPLITS ATOM

Dec 10, Stockholm The Nobel Prize for chemistry has been won by Professor Ernest Rutherford. This English scientist has shown that an atom is not the smallest particle of matter. It can be split into what he has called alpha, beta and gamma particles. Its core, or nucleus, contains a positive electric charge.

CHINA'S NEW RULER ENTHRONED

Dec 2, Peking Pu Yi has become Emperor of China. He will be three years old in February. The Empress Tzu Hsi died suddenly and mysteriously last month, a day after the unexpected death of her nephew, the Emperor.

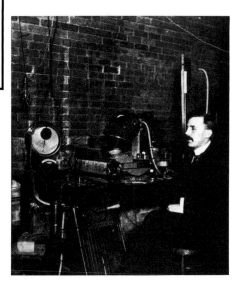

Ernest Rutherford in his laboratory.

1909

Jan 1	Old Age pensions paid in Britain
April 22	Young Turks depose the Sultan
July 25	Frenchman is first to fly the Channel
Aug 1	Spain's 'Tragic Week' of rioting
Dec 21	North Pole explorer receives medal

SOCIAL REFORM IS IN THE AIR
CASH PAID OVER THE COUNTER

Jan 1, London Post offices all over the country were visited by people of 70 and over today, to receive the first Old Age Pensions. As they were given their weekly five shillings the happy pensioners blessed the post office clerks, and 'that Lord George', as some call Mr. Lloyd George. They will spend about three shillings a week on food; the rest will pay for rent, fuel and lighting. Many of them had been facing a future in the dreaded workhouse.

BUDGET SHOCKS OPPOSITION

April 29, London As Chancellor of the Exchequer, Mr. Lloyd George presented his annual budget today. It pleases the Liberal government but has shocked Conservative MPs. They object that the rich will be taxed more heavily to pay for new social reforms, such as the new pensions. Mr. Lloyd George proposes to put a surtax on income over £5000. This will affect 10,000 people. Unearned income (from stocks and shares) will be taxed more heavily than earnings from salaries, which will again strike at the rich. Death duties on property will be doubled. Luxuries such as alcohol, cigarettes, cars and petrol will be taxed more heavily. Land owners say they will have to cut back on spending, which may put servants and tradesmen out of a job. The government thinks this is unlikely. Mr. Churchill has said Britain is the best country in the world for rich men to live in.

LORDS THROW OUT BUDGET

Nov 30, London The House of Lords has refused to pass the Liberal government's budget. Most of the Lords are wealthy landowners. The Conservative MPs are delighted. In the New Year there will be a new election, and the main issue will be the budget. If the Liberals win they may want to restrict the Lords' power so that this cannot happen again.

FRENCHMAN FLIES CHANNEL

July 25, Dover Monsieur Louis Blériot has become the first person to fly across the English Channel. He landed his 25 horsepower monoplane on the white cliffs of Dover in a high wind. He flew the 37 km (23 miles) in under 40 minutes, an average of 64 kph (40 mph). He was shown a good landing place by two men waving red flags. M. Blériot wins the *Daily Mail* prize of £1000.

TRAGIC EVENTS SHOCK SPAIN

RIOTING IN BARCELONA ALARMS GOVERNMENT

July 27, Barcelona Disturbances in this Spanish port have alarmed the King and the government. Last week women demonstrated in Madrid. Their sons and husbands had been called up because of a crisis in Spanish Morocco. They lay across the railway lines in front of the trains. Soldiers' pay is very low, and the women were afraid they would be left at home to starve.

The socialists have called a general strike, hoping that all workers in Spain will stop work. Trains taking soldiers to the troop ships have been halted. Any trams which were still running have been overturned in the streets.

CHURCH SEEN AS 'THE ENEMY'

Aug 1, Barcelona This week is being called 'Tragic Week'. The cause of the riots has shifted from the call-up to the Church. Workers blame Church leaders for their poor education, which leads to a life of poverty. They live in overcrowded housing blocks, on wages which are barely enough to keep them alive. They believe the Spanish Catholic Church is rich, and have burned 50 religious buildings, and turned the monks and nuns out into the street. The government is particularly shocked because the rioters mocked the Church by dressing up in the priests' clothing.

ALLEGED LEADER EXECUTED

Oct 13, Barcelona Spanish workers are bewildered by the news that the wealthy Francisco Ferrer has been executed. Señor Ferrer set up a number of good independent schools, which the local bishop openly condemned. The government says Ferrer was responsible for the summer riots, though he was in England at the time. The workers deny they had a leader. It seems that the government is trying to restore order through fear.

PEARY REACHES NORTH POLE

Dec 21, New York The National Geographical Society has awarded a gold medal to Commander Robert Peary. On April 6, Commander Peary, with a black American named Matthew Henson and four Eskimo guides, reached the North Pole. They travelled 1300 km (800 miles) on moving ice fields. Another explorer, Mr. Frederick Cook, claims to have reached the North Pole first, exactly a year earlier. Experts have investigated, and believe Commander Peary. They think that Mr. Cook's claim is a hoax.

"I have got the North Pole out of my system after twenty-three years of effort, hard work, disappointments, hardships, privations, more or less suffering, and some risks. I have won the last great geographical prize of the North Pole for the credit of the United States."
Robert Peary, 1910

SERBIA SETTLES FOR PEACE

March 31, Belgrade   Last year Austria took Bosnia-Herzegovina from the Turkish empire. Serbia, which neighbours Bosnia-Herzegovina, called up men for the army and prepared to go to war with Austria. In return, Austria refused to renew an important trade agreement with the Serbians unless they disarmed. The Austrians were ready to invade Serbia at that time.

Britain and France urged Serbia to give in. Reluctantly, Serbia has now agreed 'to live in future on good neighbourly terms' with the Austrian empire, and conflict was avoided.

In the Balkans, political boundaries do not follow those of national communities. There are Serbians in Bosnia, Romanians in Serbia, Bosnians in Croatia, and so on. This is bound to lead to unrest. There are rivalries between the different communities over trade, political power and natural resources.

AMERICANS SPEAK MANY LANGUAGES ...

Nov 13, Washington   The population of the United States has now reached 92 million. Over a million immigrants have been arriving every year in recent times. They come mainly from Italy, Britain, the Austrian empire, and Russia. New York has the largest number of Jewish people in any city of the world. Thousands of them escaped from persecution in Russia three years ago.

But the new life in America is not so easy. Some immigrants are illiterate and cannot speak English. They stay with others from the same country, often crowded together in poor slum housing. The more ambitious ones set to work to learn English so that they can look for well-paid jobs. Canada, Argentina, Australia and South Africa also welcome immigrants, as they have a shortage of labour.

People seem to be on the move all over the world. Whole families are buying cheap steamer tickets and taking a passage to 'a better land'.

NEWS IN BRIEF . . .

WOMEN'S WEAR IS SHORTER

Aug 1, Paris   "If you wish to see old-fashioned clothes kindly continue to frequent English [fashion] houses." So says Paris dress designer Poiret. No boned collars or sweeping trains for him! He has even done away with the tight corset. His dresses hang straight from the shoulders, and often stop above the ankle. Poiret prefers strong colours, set off by jewels and perhaps a feather or two. For playing golf many ladies wear turn-down collars and ties and a tweed cap.

Schoolgirls wear short skirts, blouses, black stockings and ankle-strap shoes. They grow their hair long and tie it back off the forehead.

Dresses from M. Poiret's collection.

TURKEY TO HAVE NEW SULTAN

April 22, Constantinople   Sultan Abdul Hamid has been deposed. He was allowed to leave by the Young Turks, who are the majority party in the new government. Officials entered his palace and removed his treasure, which they found in locked rooms. The deposed Sultan's brother is now ruling as Mahmud V.

JOAN OF ARC IS 'BLESSED'

April 18, Rome   The French have a feast day to honour Joan of Arc who was burnt at the stake by the English in 1431. Joan, a peasant girl, led 6000 soldiers against the English, who were trying to seize France. She was only 19 when she died. Today Pope Pius X has declared that she is 'blessed'. This means that one day the Catholic Church will make her a saint.

PEOPLE OF 1900-1909

Theodore Roosevelt (1858-1919)

Theodore ('Teddy') Roosevelt was an astute politician. He became Vice-President of the United States in 1900, and a year later he was sworn in as President, after President McKinley had been assassinated.

Roosevelt spoke well in Congress. He organized a treaty which led to the building of the Panama Canal. He was interested in conservation, and undertook to provide irrigation for the waterless western states. He was also a sportsman, and a writer. He loved big game hunting, and wrote books about it. Three years before he died he explored Brazil.

He was the first President to receive the Nobel Peace Prize: this was for negotiating the end of the Russo-Japanese war in 1904.

Wilbur and Orville Wright (1867-1912 and 1871-1948)

Early in their lives the brothers wanted to fly. They watched birds, they played with kites. Their father told them, 'Man will never fly. Flying is reserved for the angels.'

To start with the young men built a printing press and published two newspapers. Then they made themselves a bicycle repair shed (cycling was just becoming popular). But all the time they wanted to fly. They built model gliders and tested them in a box at one end of which was a strong fan (thus inventing the wind-tunnel).

They built themselves a full-sized glider, but it annoyed them that they had to wait for the wind to be right. Then suddenly they had the idea of making a petrol-engine turn a propellor to pull their glider along. It was this aeroplane which brought them into the news on that exciting day in 1903, when man first took to the air.

Robert Baden-Powell (1857-1941)

Robert Baden-Powell joined the army, and was in many battles in India and in Africa. During the Boer War he led the defence of Mafeking. He grouped the young boys of the town into companies, giving them useful work to do. This gave him the idea of forming the Boy Scouts, back in England, in 1907. He thought boys of all races, classes and religions should meet and talk to each other, and at the same time learn to be self-reliant and resourceful. In 1910 he founded the Girl Guides.

Helen Keller (1880-1968)

Helen Keller lived to be 88 years old, and except for her first 1½ years she saw and heard nothing. If you are blind and deaf, you cannot learn to speak by yourself. When she was seven, Anne Sullivan started to teach her. At that time Helen could feel things, but had no word for them. Anne put Helen's hand under a tap and spelt the word 'water' on the palm of her hand.

Next Anne taught her how to speak and to write. At ten Helen already had a passion for writing. *The Story of My Life* was published when she was 23, and another book in 1929. In 1953 Helen was the subject of a documentary, 'The Unconquered'. She visited Australia and Japan, and many countries in Europe, Africa and the Middle East. She worked tirelessly for other people with disabilities.

The Empress Tzu Hsi (1835-1908)

Tzu Hsi was one of the Emperor Hsien Feng's concubines. When she bore him a son she became his favourite. At the time of the Emperor's death she stole his royal seal. Without the seal, documents could not be properly signed. This stopped plotting courtiers from taking over the monarchy. Tzu Hsi governed China while her son was small. In 1875 the boy died of smallpox. She appointed her sister's son, Kuang Hsu, as the next heir. When he was 21, and could rule as Emperor, she still had great influence at court. He tried to introduce reforms, but she made him her prisoner.

Tzu Hsi encouraged the Boxer rebels because she wanted China to return to the days before Europeans interfered with its politics. She loved to act in plays. People said that she looked as though she was always on the stage.

When the time came for her to die, she saw to it that her prisoner, Kuang Hsu, died first. She appointed the two-year-old Pu Yi as her successor. He was the last Emperor of China.

For the first time ever

1900	USA	First jazz band played
		Brownie box camera on sale
		Motorbikes manufactured
	UK	A diesel motor on show
		First edition of the *Daily Express*

1901	USA	The hormone adrenalin discovered
		Cadillac motor-car manufactured
	UK	Telephone adapted as a hearing aid
		Ping-pong (table tennis) sets on sale
	Sweden	First Nobel Prizes awarded
	Germany	Mercedes motor-car manufactured

1902	France	Sci-fi film, *A Trip to the Moon*
		Press-studs invented
	USA	Pepsi-Cola on sale
		Vacuum cleaners introduced

1903	USA	Safety razors replace 'cut-throats'
		Model A Ford motor-car made
		Teddy bears on sale
	UK	First edition of the *Daily Mirror*

1904	USA	Ice cream cones sold from kiosk
	UK	Fleming invents the electronic valve
		Electrical machine for perming hair
		Rolls and Royce combine businesses
	France	First person to drive over 100 mph

1905	USA	Double-sided gramophone records
		Jukeboxes in cafés
	UK	The AA founded

1906	Germany	Photos sent by telegraph over
		1600 km (1000 miles)
	France	Grand Prix near Le Mans

THE VACUUM CLEANER

HELP!

APPLY 25 VICTORIA STREET S.W.

1907	USA	Moving picture studio at Hollywood
		Electric washing machines available
	UK	Maiden voyage of the liner *Mauretania*
		Rolls Royce Silver Ghost marketed

| 1908 | USA | First Model T Ford car |
| | | Jack Johnson is first black world heavyweight boxing champion |

1909	USA	Newsreels shown on cinema screen
		Bakelite manufactured
	UK	Selfridges store opened in London

New words and expressions

New inventions, and new habits or occupations, cause people to invent new words. They also invent new slang. These are a few of the words and phrases used for the first time in the 1900s in England and America.

aircraft	(film) location
you asked for it	novocaine
backchat	over my head
bloc	punk (nonsense)
boloney	(seat) reservation
bone-head	Scout
camber	search me!
derrick	septic tank
electrocute	sick benefit
do you get me?	we've been stung
gives me the willies	(swindled)
landing-place	to keep tabs on
het up	eternal triangle
	wisecrack

How many of these words and expressions are still used today? Do you know what they all mean?

Glossary

abandon: leave completely.
annex: take possession of territory.
anthracite: a kind of coal.
cavalry: soldiers on horseback.
controversial: causing differences of opinion.
Cossacks: horsemen in the Russian army.
cudgel: short thick stick used as weapon.
deception: being deceived, misled.
destitute: without food or shelter.
dwindle: shrink, become gradually smaller.
eruption: blowing up (of volcano).
excommunicate: cut a person off from taking part in church rituals.
flagship: ship which has the Admiral on board.
flora and fauna: plants and animals.
hoax: mischievous joke to deceive people.
horizon: line at which earth and sky seem to meet.
isolation: staying out of other countries' affairs.
khaki: grey-brown, from an Indian word meaning 'dust'.
legation: official house and offices of diplomats in a foreign country.

monopoly: enjoyed by traders with no competitors in their field.
Nonconformists: Protestants who at some time in the past broke away from the Anglican Church.
persecute: treat badly, especially on grounds of religion or race.
petrified forest: ancient trees that have become stone.
piece-work: work paid for according to the amount done.
placard: poster or card carried on a stick.
scurvy: condition caused by lack of Vitamin C.
slum: overcrowded and unhealthy back street housing.
surtax: additional tax on high income.
sweat shop: a factory or workshop where poor people worked for long hours and very little money.
trophy: prize.
vulnerable: easily hurt.
wireless telegraphy: sending signals by radio.

Further reading

The Last Czar: W.H.C. Smith. Wayland 1973
Growing up in Edwardian Britain: Nance Lui Fyson. Batsford 1986
Captain Scott: David Sweetman. Wayland 1974
The Edwardian Era: Geoffrey Trease. Batsford 1986
The Scramble for Africa: Trevor Rowell. Batsford 1986
The Edwardians: Christopher Martin. Wayland 1988

Immigrants and Emigrants: Hugh Bodley. Batsford 1982
Spotlight on the Collapse of Empires: Michael Gibson. Wayland 1986
Picture History of the 20th Century: 1900–1919: Richard Tames. Watts 1991
When I was Young: Early 20th Century: Ruth Thomson. Watts 1989